Nita Mehta

INDIAN
Favourites

Nita Mehta®

B.Sc. (Home Science), M.Sc. (Food and Nutrition), Gold Medalist

SNAB
Excellence in Books

INDIAN
Favourites

Snab Publishers Pvt Ltd
3A/3, Asaf Ali Road, New Delhi 110 002

Editorial and Marketing office
E-159, Greater Kailash II, New Delhi 110 048

Food Styling and Photography by Snab

Typesetting by National Information Technology Academy
3A/3, Asaf Ali Road, New Delhi 110 002

Recipe Development & Testing: *Creating Food Artists, not just chefs...*
Nita Mehta Creative Arts - R & D Centre
3A/3, Asaf Ali Road, New Delhi - 110 002

ISBN 978-81-7869-274-6

Revised Edition 2015

Cover Designed by:

Printed in India at Infinity Advertising Services (P) Ltd, New Delhi

Distributed by :
NITA MEHTA BOOKS
3A/3, Asaf Ali Road, New Delhi - 02

Distribution Centre :
D16/1, Okhla Industrial Area, Phase-I,
New Delhi - 110020
Tel.: 26813199, 26813200
E-mail: nitamehta.mehta@gmail.com
Website: www.nitamehta.com

Contributing Writers:
Anurag Mehta
Tanya Mehta
Subhash Mehta

Editors :
Sangeeta
Sunita

Introduction

In India, cooking is a way of expressing love. Indian food is not just a blend of spices and condiments but the food is cooked carefully, adding the right spice, the right amount of spice and at the right time. Here is a book with great recipes which will take care of all this.

Indian curries are delicious and can be prepared with just a few simple ingredients. The secret of producing these aromatic delicacies is adding the right ingredient at the right time, thus following the correct sequence of cooking.

The vegetables and meat are eaten with rice or Indian breads (*roti*). Exotic *biryaanis* and *pulaos* prepared from Indian *basmati* rice, flavoured with magical spices like fennel seeds, cinnamon sticks and cardamom pods, are all explained simply.

Special Indian sweets have been included. The Indian Ice Cream - *Kulfi* is our speciality. Mostly the sweets are milk based. Green cardamoms and saffron are used extensively in Indian desserts for flavouring.

I have tried to make the recipes as simple as possible, giving step-by-step instructions, allowing you to enjoy the exotic flavours and aroma of Indian food, any time of the week.

Nita Mehta

Contents

Snacks 11

Tandoori and Kadhai 28

Chicken and Lamb 44

Fish and Sea Food 58

Vegetarian Main Course 66

Chutneys and Pickles 78

Rice & Breads 82

Desserts and Puddings 92

Drinks

Tomato Rasam

An authentic, thin tomato soup of Southern India, delicious as an appetizer.

Serves 6-8

1 kg tomatoes - cut into 4 pieces, 3 cups water

1 tbsp oil, 2-3 whole, dry, red chillies or ½ tsp paprika

1 tsp cumin seeds (*jeera*), 1 tsp mustard seeds (*rai*), ¼ tsp asafoetida (*hing*)

a few curry leaves, ¼ tsp ground turmeric (*haldi*)

1½ tsp salt, or to taste, 1½ tsp peppercorns (*saboot kali mirch*)

1 small pod garlic, whole

1. Boil whole tomatoes with 3 cups water. Keep on low heat for about 10 minutes, till tomatoes turn soft. Remove from heat and cool. Blend to a puree.

2. Heat 1 tbsp oil. Reduce heat and fry the red chillies till they turn a shade darker. Add together — cumin seeds, mustard seeds and asafoetida. When cumin turns golden, add curry leaves.

3. Add the pureed tomatoes. Add salt and turmeric powder. Separate the flakes of garlic from the pod and crush them roughly without peeling the flakes. Separately, crush or pound the peppercorns too. Add the crushed garlic and peppercorns to the tomatoes. Boil. Simmer for 10 minutes. Remove from heat.

4. Strain. Discard the ingredients in the strainer. Serve soup garnished with coriander leaves.

Thandai

A festive drink prepared from nuts and flavourful spices blended in milk.

Serves 10-12

6 cups of milk, ½ cup almonds, 2 tbsp cashews - broken into bits

1/3 cup seeds of watermelon (*magaz*), 8 tbsp poppy seeds (*khus khus*)

15-20 peppercorns (*saboot kali mirch*), 10-12 green cardamoms (*chhoti illaichi*)

1 tbsp dried rose petals, 2 tsp fennel seeds (*saunf*)

10-12 tbsp sugar, a few strands of saffron (*kesar*) - soaked in 1 tsp water for garnishing

1. Soak almonds separately in water for 3-4 hours. Peel almonds. Soak together — watermelon seeds, poppy seeds, cashews, peppercorns, cardamoms, rose petals and fennel seeds for 3-4 hours. Strain.

2. Add the peeled almonds to the strained ingredients. Put all the soaked ingredients in a mixer grinder and grind to a paste by adding a little water or milk. The grinding of the ingredients should be done very well. Grind well to a smooth paste.

3. Add the ground ingredients to the cold milk. Add sugar and mix well. Strain the milk through a cheese cloth and discard the residue.

4. Chill the drink by adding ice. Serve garnished with soaked saffron strands and fresh rose petals.

Jeera Pani

This is predominantly a summer drink which aids digestion. A savoury tamarind and mint (pudina) cooler which is flavoured with roasted cumin seeds (jeera) and black salt. This tangy cooler can be made as peppery as you like.

Serves 4

4 cups water

4 tbsp seedless tamarind (*imli*), 4 tsp fresh lime juice

3 tbsp sugar, 1" ginger - crushed roughly

¼ cup fresh mint leaves (*pudina*) - minced

1½ tsp ground, roasted cumin (*bhuna jeera*), ½ tsp black salt (*kala namak*)

salt to taste, ½ tsp red chilli powder, or to taste, optional

1. Soak seedless tamarind in 1 cup hot water for 1 hour. Mash well. Add the remaining 3 cups water. Mash once again and strain to get tamarind water. If you are using tamarind pulp, add 4 cups of water to the pulp. If the pulp is salted, no salt is required in the *jeera pani*.

2. To the tamarind water, add all other ingredients — lime juice, crushed ginger, mint, black salt, ground roasted cumin, red chilli powder, sugar and salt to taste.

3. Mix well. Keep for 2 hours in the fridge to chill and for the flavours to penetrate. At serving time, strain through a fine sieve. Adjust seasonings. Serve garnished with a lemon slice and mint.

Pudina Lassi

This yogurt smoothie is a very popular drink in the Northern part of India, specially Punjab. There are sweet and salty versions of this Indian drink. The savoury one given here is seasoned with roasted cumin and mint whereas the delicious sweet cooler is generally flavoured with rose water and cardamoms.

Serves 4

4 tbsp finely chopped mint leaves (*pudina*)

1½ cups plain yogurt, ½ tsp rock salt (*kala namak*)

½ tsp roasted ground cumin seeds (*jeera*), ½ tsp salt, or to taste

3 cups water, 6-8 ice cubes

1. Wash and finely chop mint leaves. Put yogurt, mint, cumin seeds, rock salt and salt in a blender. Blend for a few seconds.

2. Add chilled water and ice cubes. Blend till frothy. Serve sprinkled with a pinch of ground, roasted cumin seeds and garnished with finely chopped mint.

Snacks

Paneer Rolls

These extra-crisp rolls are coated in vermicelli (seviyaan) – the filling is channa dal cooked with nuts and raisins.

Makes 12-14

2½ cups grated *paneer* (250 gm), ½ cup chopped coriander, ¾ tsp chaat masala
3 slices of brown or white bread - processed in a mixer to get fresh bread crumbs
½ tsp roasted cumin powder (*bhuna jeera*), ¾ tsp salt, ½ tsp pepper

FILLING

¼ cup yellow split peas (*channa dal*) - soaked for 2 hours & ground coarsely without water in a mixer
1 tbsp oil, 1 onion - chopped finely, 1 tsp finely chopped ginger
1 tbsp cashews (*kaju*) - chopped, 2 tbsp raisins (*kishmish*) - chopped
¼ tsp turmeric (*haldi*), ½ tsp salt, ¼ tsp red chilli powder
¼ tsp dried mango powder (*amchoor*), ½ tsp garam masala

TO COAT

½ cup very thin vermicelli (*seviyaan*) - roughly broken into small pieces by hand

1. Strain dal and roughly grind in a mixer to a coarse thick paste. Do not grind too much and make it thin and smooth.

2. Heat oil. Add onion, ginger, cashews and raisins. Cook till onions turn light golden. Add ground dal, turmeric, salt, red chilli powder, amchoor and garam masala. Stir for 1-2 minutes. Remove from heat and keep filling aside.

3. Mix grated *paneer* with coriander, chaat masala, fresh bread crumbs, roasted cumin, salt and pepper.

4. With a ball of the *paneer* mixture, make a 2" long oval roll. Flatten it to get a slight depression in the centre. Place 1 tsp of the filling in it along the length. Pick up the sides to cover the filling, such that the filling is completely covered on all sides with the *paneer* mixture. Shape to give a neat roll with slightly flattened ends.

5. Break seviyaan into 1-1½" small pieces. Spread on a plate. Take 1 cup of water separately in a shallow flat bowl (*katori*). Dip the roll in the water for a second and then immediately roll it over the seviyaan. All the sides should be completely covered with seviyaan. Keep aside to set for 15 minutes. Deep fry 2-3 pieces at a time. Serve with pudina chutney.

Fried Fish

A popular way to serve fish. Tartar sauce, although not traditionally Indian, is relished with this Indian preparation of fish. You may have it even with ordinary tomato sauce.

Serves 2-4

500 gm white fish fillet - without bones

1 tbsp lemon juice, some dry bread crumbs

MARINADE

1 tbsp ginger paste, ½ tsp salt, ½ tsp ground black pepper, ½ tsp red chilli powder

1 tsp tomato sauce, 1 egg white, a few coriander leaves - chopped

TARTAR SAUCE

½ cup mayonnaise, ¼ cup brown vinegar

1 tbsp very finely chopped cucumber, 1 tbsp very finely chopped onion

1. Rub some lemon juice on the fillets and wash fish well. Transfer it to a kitchen towel and pat dry.

2. Mix all ingredients of the marinade together in a small bowl. Transfer fish to a plate and rub marinade on the fish. Keep aside for 30 minutes.

3. At serving time, press the fish fillets on bread crumbs such that they coat the fish. Fry on medium heat till golden. Drain on absorbent paper. Serve with tomato ketchup or tartar sauce given below.

4. For tartar sauce, soak onion and cucumber in vinegar for 30 minutes. Strain the cucumber and onion to drain out the vinegar. Press gently to remove any excess liquid. Gently mix the cucumber and onion into the mayonnaise. Serve with fish fillets.

Khandavi

A very popular snack of Western India. Strips of cooked gramflour are rolled into a delicious snack. The asafoetida and mustard seeds add their delightful flavour to this light snack.

Makes 8 Rolls

½ cup gramflour (*besan*), ¾ cup yogurt, ¾ cup water

½ tbsp oil, a pinch of asafoetida (*hing*), ½ tsp salt, ¼ tsp turmeric (*haldi*)

½"/1cm piece ginger - crushed to a paste

1 green chilli - crushed to a paste

TEMPERING

2 tbsp oil, ½ tsp mustard seeds (*rai*), 1 green chilli - chopped finely, optional

2-3 tbsp chopped coriander leaves, 1 tbsp freshly grated or desiccated coconut

1. Mix together gramflour, yogurt and water well with a beater so that no lumps remain. Heat ½ tbsp oil in a heavy bottomed pan. Reduce heat. Add asafoetida. Wait for a few seconds. Add the yogurt mixture slowly, stirring continuously. Mix well.

2. Add turmeric, salt, ginger and chilli paste. Stir continuously on low heat for about 4-5 minutes till the mixture turns thick and gets cooked properly.

3. Remove from heat. Mix well and spread quickly, thinly on a plastic sheet or cling film, to a size of about 10 × 12"/25 × 30 cm. Let it cool for 5-7 minutes. Cut into thin strips, about 1"/5 cm broad. Roll each strip to make the snack. Arrange the rolls on a serving platter.

4. For tempering, heat oil. Add mustard seeds and green chilli. When the seeds stop spluttering, add coriander leaves and coconut. Mix and immediately pour all over the prepared snack.

Hare Bhare Kebabs

Makes 10

¼ cup channa ki dal (split gram)

1 bundle (600 gm) spinach - chop the leaves, very finely (6 cups)

2 tbsp oil, 3 slices bread - ground to get fresh crumbs, 2 tbsp cornflour

2 green chillies - finely chopped, ¾ tsp red chilli powder, ½ tsp garam masala

½ tsp salt or to taste, 1 tsp amchoor, 1 tbsp butter

CRUSH TOGETHER

Seeds of 2 chhoti illaichi, 2 laung, ½ tsp jeera

FILLING

½ cup grated paneer, 2 tbsp chopped coriander, salt to taste, ½ tsp bhuna jeera

1. Crush jeera, seeds of chotti illaichi and laung together.

2. Clean, wash dal. Pressure cook dal with the above crushed spices, ¼ tsp salt and ¾ cups water. After the first whistle, keep the cooker on slow fire for 15 minutes. Remove from fire and keep aside. After the pressure drops down, mash the hot dal with a karachi. If there is any water, mash the dal on fire and dry the dal as well while you are mashing it. Remove from fire.

3. Discard stem of spinach and chop leaves very finely. Wash in several changes of water. Leave the chopped spinach in the strainer for 15 minutes so that the water drains out. Heat oil in a kadahi and saute spinach leaves for 5-6 minutes till absolutely dry and well fried.

4. Add bread crumbs, cornflour, cooked spinach, chopped green chillies, salt, red chilli powder, garam masala, amchoor and butter to the mashed dal. Divide the mixture into 10 equal balls.

5. Mix grated paneer with coriander, salt and jeera. Flatten each spinach dal balls and put 1 tsp paneer filling. Cover the filling and form a flattened tikki.

6. Cook them on a tawa with 1 tbsp oil or just enough to grease the bottom of the pan. Cook till brown on both the sides. When done shift them on the sides of tawa so that they turn crisp, while more kebabs can be added to the hot oil in the centre of the tawa. Remove the kebabs on paper napkins.

7. Serve with onion rings, shredded cabbage and carrot mixed with some chat masala and lemon juice and a pinch of salt. Put a heap of this in the centre and overlap kebabs in a ring around it. Serve hari chutney with it.

Chicken Tikka

Boneless pieces of chicken are barbecued till they turn crisp on the outside and soft from inside. Chicken is marinated with cream, cheese and eggs to keep the tikkas succulent. The tikkas are flavoured with ginger and garlic pastes.

Serves 4

500 gm boneless chicken - cut into 2" pieces

1 capsicum, 1 tomato & 1 onion - cut into 1" pieces

chaat masala or lemon juice to sprinkle

FIRST MARINADE

2 tbsp vinegar, 2 tbsp ginger-garlic paste, salt to taste

SECOND MARINADE

½ cup thick yogurt - hung for 15 minutes, ¼ cup thick cream

30 gm cheddar cheese - finely grated, 1 egg

1 tbsp cornflour

1 tbsp finely chopped green chillies, optional

2 tbsp finely chopped coriander leaves

1. Wash and pat dry the chicken pieces. Marinate the chicken pieces with the first marinade — salt, vinegar and ginger-garlic paste for 30 minutes.

2. Mix yogurt, cream, cheese, egg, cornflour, green chillies and coriander in a bowl. Marinate the chicken pieces in this mixture for 2-3 hours.

3. Arrange the chicken pieces on greased skewers, with the vegetables in between the chicken pieces. Heat a gas tandoor or an oven. Place the skewers on a grill or a wire rack, brushed with some oil. Cook for about 20 minutes at 180°C, turning 1-2 times in-between. Cook till chicken turns tender.

4. Serve hot sprinkled with some lemon juice or *chaat masala* on a bed of rice.

Note: To cook the tikkas in the oven, place a drip tray under the wire rack on which the tikkas are placed, to collect the drippings.

Mutton Balls

An excellent cocktail snack. Can be served as a tea time snack too.

Serves 6

500 gm fine mince of lamb

2 tbsp garlic-ginger paste

1-2 green chillies - finely chopped

1 tsp garam masala, 4-5 tbsp gramflour (*besan*)

1 tsp ground coriander (*dhania powder*)

½-1 tsp red chilli powder

salt to taste

4 tbsp oil for shallow frying

chaat masala to sprinkle

1. Put in a strainer and gently press to drain out all the water. Check that all the water is drained out well, otherwise the balls will not bind well and tend to break while cooking.

2. Put the mince in a bowl. Add all the other ingredients. Mix and knead. Take a heaped tbsp of mince in the palm of your hand and bind the mince tightly into balls, squeezing out any excess liquid. Make balls a little big, as mince tends to shrink after cooking.

3. Take a pressure cooker, oil its bottom well. Arrange them at the bottom of the pressure cooker. Place the balls gently, over lapping one another, if short of space. Do not add water, as the mince will leave water. Pressure cook to give 2 whistles and simmer on low heat for 2 minutes. Remove from heat. Let the pressure drop by itself. Alternatively, steam balls in a steamer till cooked.

4. Gently remove the steamed meat balls. Keep aside. At serving time, add 4 tbsp oil in a non stick pan and shallow fry the steamed balls in a pan on medium heat till brown. Sprinkle *chaat masala*. Remove on a serving plate and garnish with green coriander and lemon wedges. Serve with *hari chutney*.

Note: Buy pre-washed mince. If at all you need to wash it, put mince in a strainer and wash it with some water in the strainer.

Achaari Tikke

Kebabs that melt in your mouth.

Serves 6

400 gm mushrooms - boiled in water with a pinch of turmeric (*haldi*) for 3-4 minutes

400 gm *paneer* - cut into 1½" pieces

4 tbsp ready-made mango pickle (*achaar*) - discard any hard portion, chop finely and grind to a smooth paste in a mixer

2 cups yogurt - hang in a muslin cloth for 1 hour, 3 tsp garlic paste, 2 tsp ginger paste

¾ tsp black salt (*kala namak*), ½ tsp salt, ¼ tsp white pepper powder

2 tbsp lemon juice, 1 tsp chaat masala, 1½ tsp cumin (*jeera*) powder

¼ cup grated processed cheese, 1 tbsp butter

¾ tsp pomegranate seed (*anardana*) powder

3 tbsp gramflour (*besan*), 3 tbsp mustard oil

TEMPERING

3 tbsp mustard oil, 2 tsp degi red chilli

1 tsp fennel (*saunf*), ½ tsp onion seeds (*kalaunji*)

¼ tsp fenugreek seeds (*methi dana*), ½ tsp mustard seeds (*sarson*)

1. Heat mustard oil in a pan. Add gramflour and roast on low heat for about 4-5 minutes till gramflour just starts to change colour and turns fragrant. Keep aside.

2. In a flat dish place cheese. Rub with the palm till smooth. Add yogurt, mix thoroughly until cheese is smoothly mixed with the yogurt.

3. Add ginger, garlic paste, salt, black salt, lemon juice, pickle paste, white pepper powder, chaat masala, cumin powder, pomegranate seed powder and roasted gramflour along with the oil. Mix well till smooth.

4. Take a small pan, heat 3 tbsp mustard oil. Remove from fire. Add fennel, onion seeds, fenugreek seeds, mustard seeds and degi mirch. Put this mixture into the yogurt marinade. Mix.

5. Add *paneer* and mushrooms in the marinade. Mix well. Arrange *paneer* and mushrooms alternately on well greased skewers, or simply place them on a grill rack covered with aluminium foil. Grease foil before placing the tikkas.

6. Preheat oven to 180°C or a tandoor on moderate flame. Cook for 15 minutes in the preheated oven till well-browned and cooked. Serve hot.

Shami Kebabs

Discs of lamb mince mixed with some yellow split peas.

Serves 8

COOK TOGETHER

500 gm mutton mince (*keema*)

¼ cup yellow split peas (*channe ki dal*) - soaked for 15 minutes in water & drained

1 onion - sliced (½ cup), 1 tbsp chopped garlic, 2"/5 cm piece ginger - chopped

2 tsp coriander seeds (*saboot dhania*)

1 tsp cumin seeds (*jeera*), 3-4 cloves (*laung*)

2 green cardamoms (*chhoti illaichi*)

2 brown cardamoms (*moti illaichi*)

½" stick cinnamon (*dalchini*)

1 bay leaf (*tej patta*)

4-5 peppercorns (*saboot kali mirch*)

2-3 dry, whole red chillies, salt to taste

½ cup water

1. Wash the mince and drain out the water well through a strainer. Press well to squeeze out all the water.

2. Add all the ingredients to the mince and cook in a heavy bottomed pan on medium heat till done or pressure cook to give 2 whistles. Keep on low heat for 2 minutes. Remove from heat.

3. When the pressure drops, uncover the pressure cooker. If there is any water left, keep the cooker on heat to dry the water. If the mince is wet, the kebabs break while frying, so dry it well.

4. Dry grind the dried minced meat either on stone grinder or in a food processor till smooth without adding any water while grinding.

5. To prepare the kebabs, make tiny balls. Flatten them into small discs. Shallow fry in oil in a non stick pan on medium heat, till brown on both sides. Serve.

Murg Kali Mirch

Delicious dry chicken - can be served as the main dish or a snack. You can also put this in the makhani gravy along with the butter in which it is cooked.

Serves 5-6

1 chicken (800 gm) - cut into 12 pieces - make incisions

6-7 tbsp butter (preferably Amul),2 tbsp grated ginger

1 tsp salt, 1¼ tsp freshly ground pepper

1 tbsp lemon juice (adjust to taste)

some fresh coriander - chopped

4-5 saboot kali mirch (peppercorns) - coarsely powdered

1. Heat butter on medium flame. Add grated ginger. Fry on medium heat till slightly brown. (If the heat is too much, the butter will burn).

2. Add chicken, salt and pepper and fry for about 5 minutes, till chicken changes colour.

3. Lower heat, cover and let it cook for about 15 minutes or till chicken is tender.

4. Increase heat, add lemon juice and cook till dry.

5. Sprinkle coarsely pounded pepper and fresh coriander and mix well. Serve hot.

Tandoori
&
Kadhai

Balti Aloo

A perfect combination of five seeds are popped into hot oil to impart all their flavour. Fresh coriander leaves enhance the taste and look of this humble potato dish.

Serves 4

4 medium (375 gm) potatoes, 2 medium onions - sliced (¾ cup)

3 tbsp oil

½ tsp cumin seeds (*jeera*), ½ tsp fennel seeds (*saunf*), ¼ tsp nigella seeds (*kalonji*)

¼ tsp mustard seeds (*rai*), 2 pinches of fenugreek seeds (*methi dana*)

4-6 flakes garlic - crushed (1 tsp) 1"/2.5 cm piece ginger - cut into match sticks

½ tsp turmeric (*haldi*), 1-2 dry, red chillies, a few curry leaves or fresh coriander leaves

salt to taste, 1 tsp *chaat masala*

1. Peel, wash and cut potatoes into ¼" thick, round slices.

2. Heat oil in a non stick wok or a skillet. Reduce heat, collect all seeds — cumin, fennel, onion, mustard and fenugreek seeds, and add all together to the oil. Cook for ½ minute till the fennel seeds start changing colour.

3. Add garlic and ginger, stir fry for 1 minute. Add onions, stir fry until onions turn light golden. Add turmeric and dry red chillies. Stir. Add fresh coriander or curry leaves. Stir.

4. Add potatoes and salt. Mix well. Keeping the heat very low, cover tightly with a lid, and cook for 10-12 minutes or until the potatoes are tender. Uncover and add *chaat masala*. Adjust the seasonings. Transfer to a serving platter and serve hot as a side dish.

Tandoori Chicken

An all time favourite of not only Punjabis but of all the people fond of good food.

Serves 4-5

1 small sized chicken (800 gm) - cut into 8 pieces

1 cup thick yogurt (*curd*) - hang in a muslin cloth for ½ hour

2 tbsp plain flour (*maida*), 2 tbsp oil

3 tsp ginger-garlic paste, a pinch of orange red colour

1 tbsp dry fenugreek (*kasoori methi*) - dry roasted on a *tawa* for 2 minutes and crushed to a powder

½ tsp cumin (*jeera*) powder, ½ tsp coriander (*dhania*) powder

½ tsp garam masala powder, 2 tsp tandoori masala

1½ tsp amchoor powder, 1 tsp salt, 1 tsp red chilli powder

4 tbsp oil for basting (pouring on top)

1. Mix yogurt, flour, colour and all other ingredients. Add enough colour to get a bright orange colour.

2. Wash chicken. Squeeze out all excess water. Pat dry on a clean kitchen towel.

3. Marinate chicken in the yogurt mixture for 2-3 hours in the refrigerator.

4. Rub the wire rack of the oven with oil and place the marinated chicken on it, so that the extra marinade can drip down from the grill rack. If the chicken is placed in a dish or a tray, the extra marinade and liquid keep collecting around the chicken pieces and hence they do not turn dry and crisp.

5. Cook for 8-10 minutes in an oven at 180°C. Overturn again, baste (pour) with oil and cook for another 10-12 minutes or till tender and crisp.

6. Serve hot garnished with onion rings.

Note:

♦ Instead of a full chicken only drumsticks (legs) can be made. They are called tangdi kebabs. After grilling, wrap a piece of aluminium foil at the end of each leg. Besides looking nice, it is also convenient for holding and eating the chicken leg.

♦ Boneless chicken cut into 1½"-2" pieces can be cooked in a similar manner to get chicken tikka.

♦ The tandoori chicken can be added to an onion-tomato masala for a tikka masala dish.

Kadhai Murg

A semi - dry preparation of chicken, flavoured with fenugreek and coriander.

Serves 4-6

1 medium sized (800 gm) chicken - cut into 12 pieces, 6-7 tbsp oil

1 tbsp coriander seeds (*saboot dhania*)

3 whole, dry red chillies, ½ tsp fenugreek seeds (*methi dana*)

3 large onions - cut into slices, 15-20 flakes garlic - crushed & chopped (2 tbsp)

1" piece of ginger - crushed to a paste (1 tbsp)

4 large tomatoes - chopped

½ cup ready-made tomato puree or ¾ cup homemade puree

1 tsp red chilli powder, 1 tsp ground coriander powder (*dhania*)

2 tsp salt, or to taste, ¼ tsp amchoor, ½ tsp garam masala

½ cup chopped green coriander, 1 capsicum - cut into slices

1" piece ginger - cut into match sticks

1-2 green chillies - cut into long slices, ½ cup cream, optional

1. Put coriander seeds and whole red chillies on a *tawa*. Keep on fire and roast lightly till it just starts to change colour. Do not make them brown. Remove from fire.

2. Crush the coriander seeds on a *chakla-belan* (rolling board and pin) to split the seeds. Keep red chillies whole. Keep aside.

3. Heat oil in a *kadhai*. Reduce heat. Add fenugreek seeds and whole red chillies and stir for a few seconds till fenugreek seeds turns golden.

4. Add onion and cook on medium heat till light brown. Add garlic and stir for 1 minute. Add ginger paste. Add the coriander seeds, red chilli powder and coriander powder.

5. Add chicken and bhuno for 10 minutes on high flame, stirring well so that chicken attains a nice golden brown colour.

6. Add chopped tomatoes. Cook for 4-5 minutes. Add salt, amchoor and garam masala. Cover and cook for 15-20 minutes or till tender, stirring occasionally.

7. Add tomato puree and chopped green coriander. Cook for 5 minutes.

8. Add the capsicum, ginger match sticks and green chilli slices. Mix well.

9. Reduce heat. Add cream. Mix well for 2-3 minutes and serve hot.

Tandoori Fish

Delicious, succulent fish. Can be served as a snack or with the main meal.

Serves 3-4

500 gm fish - cut into 5-6 pieces, preferably boneless and skinless

3 tbsp gramflour (*besan*), 1 tbsp lemon juice

½ tsp salt, ½ tsp red chilli powder

MARINADE

2½ tsp Kashmiri red chilli powder (*degi mirch*)

½ tsp black cumin (*shah jeera*), 1 tsp ginger paste, 1 tsp garlic paste

½ tsp tandoori masala, ½ tsp garam masala powder

1½ tsp amchoor, 1 tsp coriander powder (*dhania*)

2 tbsp lemon juice, ¼ tsp chaat masala, 1¼ tsp salt

BASTING

4 tbsp melted butter mixed with ¼ tsp black cumin (*shah jeera*)

1. Rub the fish well with 3 tbsp gramflour and 2 tbsp lemon juice to remove the fishy odour. Keep aside for 15 minutes. Wash well and pat dry on a kitchen towel. Prick fish all over with a fork or give shallow cuts with a knife.

2. Mix all ingredients given under marinade. Rub the marinade well all over the fish pieces and let it marinate for 2-3 hours.

3. Heat an electric oven to 160°C or a gas tandoor on gas at low heat. Grease the wire rack and place fish pieces on it. Let it cook for 8-10 minutes.

4. Baste (pour) with melted butter mixed with black cumin. Cook again for 5-6 minutes till well cooked and crisp. The time of cooking will depend on the thickness of the fish and may vary a little.

5. Sprinkle chaat masala and serve hot with dahi pudina chutney and sirke waale pyaaz.

Note:

♦ A small fish (pomfret) can be made whole in this way.

♦ While grilling, always place fish pieces (or a whole fish) on a rack with the drip tray below it as it will leave some liquid which will drip down. If the fish is placed on a baking tray, the water will remain around the fish and hence make it soggy and it will not get crisp.

Tandoori Cauliflower

Whole cauliflower is baked with a ginger-garlic flavoured yogurt masala stuffed within the florets. Onion rings and fresh coriander topping adds to the taste.

Serves 8

3 small cauliflowers, each about 350 gm

MARINADE

1½ cups thick yogurt - hung for 30 minutes to give about ¾ cup hung yogurt

2 tbsp ginger-garlic paste

2 tsp *tandoori masala*

¼ tsp salt, or to taste, 2 pinches of turmeric for colour, ½ tsp paprika or degi mirch

2 tbsp oil

TOPPING

2 tbsp oil

4-5 small onions - cut into fine rings (1 cup), ¼ cup tomato puree

3-4 tbsp chopped fresh coriander, 1 green chilli - deseeded and chopped

salt to taste, 1 tsp *tandoori masala*

1. Boil 5-6 cups of water in a large pan with 2 tsp salt. Add the cauliflowers to the boiling water. Cook till it turns barely tender. Do not cook for too long. Remove from water and dry well on a clean kitchen napkin. Keep aside.

2. Mix all ingredients of the marinade in a bowl. Apply the marinade on the cauliflower, inserting some marinade inside the florets. Turn the cauliflower and insert some marinade from the backside also. Marinate the cauliflowers for at least 1 hour.

3. Place the marinated cauliflowers on a grill rack and cook in a hot oven at 200°/400°F till crisp and golden. Remove and keep on the serving platter.

4. To prepare the topping, heat 2 tbsp oil in pan. Add onion rings. When they start turning brown, add tomato puree. Stir. Add fresh coriander, green chillies and *tandoori masala*. Adjust salt and seasonings.

5. To serve, spread some onion topping on the grilled cauliflowers. Heat in a microwave or an oven. Serve hot with rice or bread.

Broccoli Spears

Broccoli florets with long stalks are flavoured with carom seeds and barbecued.

Serves 4

500 gm (2 medium heads) broccoli - cut into medium sized florets with long stalks

2 tsp salt, 1 tsp sugar

1ST MARINADE

juice of 1 lemon (3-4 tsp)

¾ tsp carom seeds (*ajwain*)

1 tsp salt and ½ tsp red chilli powder

2ND MARINADE

1 cup thick yogurt - hung for 15 minutes or more

½ cup thick cream

2 tsp ginger paste

½ tsp red chilli paste, optional

¾ tsp salt, 1 tsp *tandoori masala*

1. Boil 5-6 cups of water in a large pan. Add 2 tsp salt and 1 tsp sugar to the water. Add broccoli pieces to the boiling water. Boil. Keep on boiling for 2 minutes. Drain. Wipe the pieces well with a clean kitchen towel till well dried.

2. Spread the broccoli on a flat plate and sprinkle the ingredients of the 1st marinade. Marinate the broccoli for 15 minutes.

3. Drain the broccoli of any excess liquid. Mix all the ingredients of the 2nd marinade. Add the broccoli to it and mix well. Check the salt and add more if needed. Keep in the refrigerator till the time of serving.

4. Brush the grill of the oven or gas tandoor with some oil. Place the broccoli spears on it and barbecue them in a gas oven for 10 minutes or grill in a preheated electric oven only for 10 minutes. Do not over grill it, turns too dry. Serve hot as a side dish.

Hyderabadi Okra

Coconuts are abundant in the Southern part of India and so they are included in all South Indian delicacies. Freshly grated coconut gives a slight crunchy texture as well as a sweetish flavour to the food.

Serves 4

250 gm okra (*bhindi*), ¼ of a fresh coconut, 4-5 cashews (*kaju*), 4 tbsp oil

½ tsp black mustard seeds (*sarson*), ½ tsp cumin seeds (*jeera*), 10-15 curry leaves

1 small onion - finely chopped (1/3 cup), 2 small tomatoes - finely chopped (¾ cup)

½ tsp chilli powder, ¼ tsp turmeric (*haldi*), 1/3 cup yogurt, ¾ tsp salt, or to taste

1. Grind together fresh coconut and cashews to a paste. Keep aside.

2. Remove only the tip of the stalk end of each okra. Cut lengthways into two. Heat 3 tbsp oil in a wok and stir fry okra for about 10 minutes on medium heat till done. Do not cover while cooking.

3. Heat 1 tbsp oil. Remove from heat. Collect mustard and cumin seeds and add to the hot oil together. Fry on low heat till cumin changes colour.

4. Add curry leaves and onions and fry until onions turn golden. Add tomatoes, chilli powder, turmeric and salt. Stir fry till tomatoes turn dry and oil separates.

5. Add yogurt, a little at a time, stirring continuously. Bring to a boil, stirring continuously. Stir fry until dry and oil separates. Add coconut-cashew paste. Stir for a minute. Add okra, mix well. Serve hot with any type of bread.

Kadhai Paneer

Fenugreek seeds and garlic are used to flavour this quick, yet exotic dish of paneer. Experiment this recipe with fried potato fingers as a substitute of paneer to get kadhai aloo.

Serves 6

250 gm *paneer* - cut into long thin fingers

2 green capsicums - cut into thin long pieces (1 cup)

2 dry, red chillies, 4 tbsp oil

1½ tsp coriander seeds (*saboot dhania*), ¼ tsp fenugreek seeds (*methi dana*)

½ tbsp crushed garlic, 1 tbsp ginger-chopped

3 tomatoes - chopped (1½ cups)

¾ tsp salt, or to taste

GARNISHING

1"/2.5 cm piece ginger - finely shredded

1. Coarsely grind dry, red chillies and coriander seeds together. Keep aside. Heat oil. Reduce heat. Add fenugreek seeds. Wait for a few seconds till they turn brown.

2. Add crushed garlic and cook till light brown. Add ground red chillies and coriander seeds. Stir. Add chopped ginger. Cook for 30 seconds.

3. Add chopped tomatoes, stir fry for about 5-7 minutes till oil separates. Add salt and green capsicums. Stir for a minute.

4. Add *paneer*. Cook for 2-3 minutes. Transfer to a serving dish. Garnish with shredded ginger. Serve hot with *paranthas*.

Badami Tangri

Serves 5

5 drumsticks (500 gm chicken legs)

1ST MARINADE

2 tbsp lemon juice

1 tbsp oil

½ tsp salt

½ tsp red chilli powder

2ND MARINADE

½ cup yogurt (*curd*) - hang for 30 minutes

2 tbsp oil, 2 tbsp ginger-garlic paste

8-10 almonds - ground to a powder

¼ cup thick cream

¾ tsp salt

1 tbsp cornflour

2 tsp dry fenugreek leaves (*kasoori methi*)

2 tbsp chopped coriander

1. Wash & pat dry the chicken legs. Make 2 light cuts/incisions on each drumstick.

2. Marinate chicken with 1st marinade for 30 minutes.

3. Mix ingredients of 2nd marinade in a bowl. Add only chicken pieces discarding the liquid. Marinate for 2-3 hours in the fridge.

4. To serve, grease a flat borosil dish. Place the chicken on it. Cook in a microwave oven on combination mode (microwave 540W + Grill) for 8 minutes or till golden. Turn side and smear the remaining marinade. Cook for 4 minutes on the same combination mode. If using an OTG, cook at 160°C for 15-20 minutes till soft. Serve with pudina chutney.

Chicken & Lamb

Chicken Curry

*Flavoured with cumin, garlic and ginger, this curry is delicious
with rice as well as any bread.*

Serves 4-6

750 gm boneless chicken

5 tbsp oil

1 bay leaf (*tej patta*), 1-2 black cardamoms (*moti illaichi*)

10-15 cashews (*kaju*) - ground to a paste with a little water

3 onions - finely chopped (1½ cups), 1 tbsp ginger paste, 2 tbsp garlic paste

1 tsp cumin seeds (*jeera*), 2 tomatoes - chopped (1 cup)

½ cup thick yogurt - beaten well till smooth, ½ cup milk

1 tsp each chilli powder & garam masala, salt to taste

2 tbsp chopped, fresh coriander

1. Soak cashews in warm water for 10-15 minutes and grind to a very smooth paste with a little water. Heat oil in a heavy bottomed pan. Add a bay leaf and cumin. Wait for a few seconds till cumin turns golden.

2. Add the chopped onions and stir fry till onions turn light brown. Add ginger and garlic paste and stir fry for 1 minute.

3. Add tomatoes and stir fry till dry and oil separates. Add the chicken pieces and stir fry on high heat for about 5 minutes or till the chicken is half cooked and the water evaporates. Add cashew paste, chilli powder, salt and garam masala.

4. Add the yogurt mixture to the chicken, stir for a few minutes till the yogurt turns dry and blends well with the masala. Add ½ cup milk. Stir. Cook covered on low heat till the chicken is done and the masala coats the pieces. Serve hot with *naan* or *roti*.

Hyderabadi Mutton Korma

Serves 4-5

1 kg mutton with bones

WHOLE GARAM MASALA

8 green cardamoms (*illaichi*), 6 cloves (*laung*), 3 bay leaves (*tej patte*)

8 tbsp oil

3 large onions cut into 4 pieces - boil in 1 cup water for 10 minutes, drain and grind in mixer to paste (boiled onion paste)

3 tsp ginger paste, 4 tbsp garlic paste, 1 tsp red chilli powder, 3 tsp coriander powder

½ tsp white pepper powder, 1 tsp garam masala powder

5-6 tbsp thick cream, ¼ cup milk, ¼ tsp saffron, 1½ tsp salt

MIX TOGETHER

200 gm (1 cup) yogurt (*dahi*)

8 almonds and 3 tbsp magaz seeds-grind in mixer to powder

GRIND TOGETHER

¼ tsp javitri powder, ¼ tsp green cardamom powder

FOR GARNISH

¼ tsp kesar, 2 tbsp chopped green coriander

1. Clean and wash the mutton and cut into 1½" cup all bones cut slantly.

2. Heat oil in a thick bottom pan, add whole garam masala and fry till it begin to crackle.

3. Add onion paste and fry on medium heat till brown in colour for (10-12 minutes.) Add ginger + garlic paste. Cook for 2 minutes.

4. Add mutton and stir fry for 5-7 minutes. Sprinkle a little water if it sticks to the bottom.

5. Take it off the fire. Let it cool completely. Add curd mix with almond powder and magaz powder. Return to low heat and bring to boil. Add 2½ cups of water. Bring to boil again and simmer. Covered till meat is tender. Remove from fire. Add cream mix well.

6. Add javitri and cardamom powdered. Dissolve saffron in warm milk and add to the mutton garnish with chopped coriander.

Butter Chicken

Chicken cooked in a fragrant red coloured sauce made in butter.
Relished by almost everyone!

Serves 6

1 tandoori chicken (page 34) - cut into 8 pieces

GRAVY

500 gm tomatoes - grind to a puree

50 gm salted butter, 2 tbsp ginger-garlic paste

¼ cup cashews (*kaju*) - soaked in hot water for 15 minutes

¼ tsp degi mirch

1¼ cups milk, 100 gm thin fresh cream (½ cup)

½ tsp garam masala, salt to taste, ¼ tsp sugar

1 tsp *tandoori masala*

1 bay leaf (*tej patta*)

1. Soak cashews in hot water for 15 minutes. Drain and grind to a very fine paste with a little water.

2. Melt butter in nonstick pan. Add a bay leaf. Wait for a few seconds. Add ginger-garlic paste, cook until liquid evaporates and the paste just changes colour. Add freshly pureed tomatoes, cook until the puree turns absolutely dry and fat separates.

3. Add cashew paste, stir for a few seconds. Add 2 tbsp cream. Add degi mirch to give a bright red colour, (a few drops of orange red colour can also be added). Cook on medium heat till fat separates.

4. Remove from heat. Add milk, and enough water (about 1 cup) to get a thick curry. Mix well. Return to heat. Bring to a boil, stirring constantly. Cover and simmer for 5-7 minutes till the gravy turns to a bright red colour and fat surfaces.

5. Remove from heat and stir in rest of the cream, stirring continuously. Add garam masala, *tandoori masala* and sugar to taste.

6. Add *tandoori* chicken. Give one or two quick boils on low heat and heat through. Remove from heat. Garnish with 1 tbsp of fresh cream and slit green chillies. Serve hot with *nan or paranthas*.

Keema Kofta

Stuffed minced meat balls cooked in a delicious creamy gravy.

Makes 15 koftas

KOFTA

500 gm keema (minced meat), 4 tbsp oil, 1 onion - finely chopped
8 finely chopped flakes of garlic, 1 tbsp grated ginger, 2 green chillies - finely chopped
½ tsp red chilli powder (*degi mirch*), 1½ tsp salt, 1 egg and 1 yolk, ¼ tsp garam masala
4 tbsp chopped mixed nuts (*badam, kishmish, pista*)

GRAVY

4 tbsp oil, 2 onions - ground to a paste, 1 tsp finely chopped garlic
½ tsp red chilli powder, 1½ tbsp coriander powder, 1 tsp salt, 1 tbsp ginger paste
2 large tomatoes, 2½ cups water or stock
½ cup cream, 1 tbsp finely chopped fresh coriander leaves

1. For the koftas, heat oil, add onions and garlic till golden brown.

2. Add minced meat, ginger, green chillies, red chilli powder and salt. Mix well. Cook covered on slow fire for 5-7 minutes till the juices dry up. Remove from the fire. Cool. Grind to a paste. Add chopped nuts.

3. Beat eggs and mix with the mince. Add ½ tsp garam masala too.

4. Divide mince into 15 equal parts. With the help of a little water shape it into a round ball of the size of walnut. Fry in hot oil till golden in colour.

5. For gravy, chopped tomatoes roughly. Boil in ½ cup water for 7-8 minutes. Remove from fire and cool. Grind in a mixer to a puree. Strain the puree.

6. Heat oil in a *kadhai* & fry the onions till golden brown. Add garlic, red chilli powder, coriander powder & salt. Cook for a minute. Add ginger and mix.

7. Add tomatoes. Bhuno well for 5-7 minutes till the tomatoes blend well. Add water or stock and simmer on slow fire for about 15 minutes.

8. Add fried koftas to gravy. Allow them to simmer for 10 minutes or till they are soft and swollen and the gravy is reduced to half. Keep aside till serving time.

9. At serving time, heat the koftas in gravy and reduce heat. Pour in the cream and mix. Remove from fire. Transfer to a serving dish.

10. Sprinkle ¼ tsp garam masala and finely chopped coriander leaves.

Rogan Josh–Kashmiri Lamb Curry

A spicy thin mutton curry, cooked with fennel seeds and ground ginger.

Serves 4

500 gm lamb (*mutton*)

½ cup yogurt, ¼ tsp asafoetida (*hing*)

4 tbsp oil

1 onion - ground to a paste (½ cup)

salt to taste

GRIND TO A FINE POWDER

2 tsp fennel seeds (*saunf*), seeds of 3 brown cardamoms (*moti illaichi*)

1 tsp cumin seeds (*jeera*), 2 cloves (*laung*)

3-4 dry, red chillies, 1 tbsp ginger powder (*sonth*)

Note: Onion is optional, it is added so that the gravy does not remain too thin.

1. Wash and pat dry mutton on a kitchen towel.

2. Heat oil in a pressure cooker or a deep pan. Add asafoetida powder.

3. Add dry meat and stir fry till the mutton turns dry and all the water evaporates. Stir fry further till the mutton turns golden brown and gives a well fried look.

4. Add onion paste and stir fry for 2 minutes on medium heat.

5. Mix the yogurt with the freshly ground spices and add it to the mutton. Add salt. Stir fry for 5-7 minutes till the yogurt blends well and turns dry.

6. Add 2 cups of water, pressure cook to give 2 whistles. Reduce heat and pressure cook further for 4 minutes. If you are not using a pressure cooker, add extra water and cook covered on low heat till the mutton gets done. Check for tenderness. Serve hot with rice.

Mutton Vindaloo

Vinegar and garlic are the main ingredients of this Goanese mutton curry. Vindaloos are generally very hot, but the chillies have been reduced to give you a mild curry.

Serves 4

500 gm mutton - cut into 1"/2.5 cm pieces, 2 potatoes - cut into 4 pieces

2 tomatoes - blanched in hot water, peeled & chopped

4 tbsp ghee

GRIND TOGETHER

¼ tsp cumin seeds (*jeera*), 1 stick cinnamon (*dalchini*)

1 tsp red chillies, ¼ tsp mustard seeds (*rai*), 1 tsp chopped garlic, 1 tsp chopped ginger

½ cup sliced onion, salt to taste, 3-4 tbsp vinegar

1. Clean, wash and cut mutton into 1" pieces. Grind the spices, ginger, garlic and onions using some vinegar to a paste. Marinate mutton with this paste and keep aside for 2-3 hours.

2. Heat oil and fry the meat well. Add remaining vinegar and more water. Cook meat on a slow heat, when meat is three-fourths cooked.

3. Add quartered potatoes, blanched and chopped tomatoes. Remove from heat when meat is tender.

Saag Chicken

The addition of fresh spinach to chicken makes the dish healthier as well as tastier.

Serves 6-8

1 chicken (750 gm) - cut into 8 pieces

500 gm spinach (*paalak*)

3 onions - chopped finely (1½ cups)

3 tbsp ginger-garlic paste

1 large tomato - chopped (¾ cup)

½ cup thick yogurt - beaten well till smooth

1 tsp garam masala, 1 tsp red chilli powder, salt to taste

½ cup milk or water

4-5 tbsp oil

2 tbsp cream to garnish, optional

a few ginger juliennes to garnish

1. Cut the stems of spinach and chop the leaves finely. Wash leaves in plenty of water, changing water several times.

2. Heat oil in a heavy bottomed pan. Add onions. Cook till light brown.

3. Add the ginger-garlic paste. Cook for 1 minute. Add tomato. Cook for 1 minute, till they turn mushy.

4. Add yogurt, salt, chilli powder, garam masala and cook stirring continuously on high heat till oil separates.

5. Drain out all the excess water from spinach and add to the masala. Cook on high heat till all the water evaporates.

6. Now add the washed chicken pieces and stir fry on high heat, stirring constantly.

7. Cook till water evaporates and the masala coats the chicken pieces. Add milk or water. Reduce heat. Cover and cook till the chicken is tender.

8. Remove cover and cook again for 2 to 3 minutes or till the chicken pieces get coated with the spinach masala. Garnish with ginger juliennes and cream. Serve hot with any bread.

Dal with Mutton

This mutton lentil curry is a Hyderabadi speciality which is lightly soured with tamarind. The lentils absorb the taste of the mutton with which they are cooked.

Serves 6

½ kg mutton

¾ cup split red lentils (*dhuli masoor dal*)

2 tsp melon seeds (*magaz*) - crush or grind in mixer

2 medium onions - thinly sliced, 1 tsp ginger paste, 1½ tsp garlic paste

1 tsp red chilli powder, ½ tsp turmeric (*haldi*) powder, ½ tsp black cumin (*shah jeera*)

½" cinnamon stick (*dalchini*), 2 green cardamoms (*illaichi*), 4 cloves (*laung*)

1 lemon size ball of tamarind - soaked in ½ cup hot water for 15 minutes & strained

½ cup chopped green coriander, 2 green chillies - keep whole

¼ cup oil, 2 tsp salt or to taste

TEMPERING (*BAGHAAR*)

4 dry red chillies, 15-20 curry leaves, 4 tbsp finely chopped garlic

½ tsp cumin seeds (*jeera*), 1 tsp fenugreek seeds (*methi dana*), 2 tbsp oil

1. Pressure cook lentils in 2 cups of water with ½ tsp salt and ¼ tsp turmeric powder to give 1 whistle. Remove from fire and let the pressure drop by itself.

2. Heat oil in a pressure cooker, add black cumin seeds, cinnamon, cloves and cardamom. Cook for 1 minute till spices darken a little. Add onions & cook on medium flame till light brown, add ginger and garlic and cook for 1 minute. Add salt, turmeric, red chilli powder and the ground melon seeds, fry for a few seconds, sprinkle a little water and cook for 1-2 minutes till well blended.

3. Add meat and fry for 6-8 minutes on medium flame till the water dries up and the meat acquires a well fried look. Add ¾-1 cup water for the meat to become tender and pressure cook first on high flame till pressure develops for 2-3 minutes and then reduce heat. Keep on medium flame for 6-8 minutes or till the meat is tender. Remove from fire and wait for the pressure to drop by itself. Check meat for tenderness.

4. Add the prepared boiled lentils, tamarind water, green chillies and coriander and simmer for about 5-7 minutes. Transfer to a serving dish.

5. For baghaar, heat oil. Add all the ingredients of the baghaar. When the red chillies darken, add the baghaar to the hot dalcha. Cover immediately. Serve.

Fish & Sea Food

Tomato Fish

A delicious way of preparing fish in a slightly sweet and sour tomato sauce with diced capsicum.

Serves 6

500 gm fish - cut into 2" pieces

3 medium onions - chopped finely (1½ cups)

1 green capsicum - chopped finely (½ cup)

3 tbsp oil

¾ cup tomato puree, 1 tsp chill sauce, 1 tbsp vinegar

½ tsp sugar, ¾ tsp salt, or to taste

2 tsp cornflour

1. Heat oil in a pan. Add onions. Stir fry till transparent. Add green capsicum. Saute for a few seconds. Add tomato puree, chilli sauce, salt, sugar and vinegar. Mix well.

2. Add fish in a single layer over the masala, without overlapping. Cook uncovered for 6-7 minutes on low heat. (Overturn the pieces of fish after 3-4 minutes). Cook till fish is properly cooked.

3. Remove the fish pieces with a slotted spoon on to a serving dish. To the gravy in the pan, add cornflour dissolved in ¾ cup of water. Give one boil. Simmer for 2-3 minutes. Pour over the fish. Serve tomato fish with rice.

Bengali Fish Curry

Serves 4

300 gm fish - cut into 1½" flat pieces

1 tbsp lemon juice

½ tsp salt, ½ tsp turmeric (*haldi*)

4 tbsp oil

¼ tsp chilli powder

1 tbsp chopped coriander

MUSTARD PASTE (GRIND)

4 tsp yellow mustard (*peeli sarson*)

2 dry, red chillies - deseed

1 onion - chopped finely

¼ tsp salt

2-3 tbsp water to grind

1. Rub lemon juice, salt and turmeric on fish. Keep aside for 10 minutes. Wash fish, pat dry.

2. Heat 2 tbsp oil in a pan. Place fish in the pan in a single layer. Cook on medium heat for about 1½ minutes. Turn side and cook for the same time, so that both sides of the fish are golden and the fish is cooked.

3. Heat 2 tbsp oil in a *kadhai*. Add the mustard paste. Stir for 3 minutes. Add ½ cup water. Bring to a boil and then cook on low heat for 2 minutes.

4. Add fish. Mix well. Add ¼ tsp chilli powder. Sprinkle chopped coriander. Keep aside till serving time. To serve heat on low flame for 2 minutes.

Goan Fish Curry

Another landscape, another cuisine – this curry has tamarind and coconut milk, curry leaves and black mustard seeds.

Serves 4

400 gm of any firm white fish - cut into 2" pieces

4 tbsp oil

2-3 green chillies - deseeded and sliced

1 tsp red chilli powder, 2 tsp coriander (*dhania*) powder

½ tsp garam masala, 1 tsp salt

2 cups thick coconut milk

2 tbsp tamarind (*imli*) pulp, optional

1 cup water

PASTE

1 medium onion, 2½" piece of ginger, 8-10 flakes of garlic

TEMPERING (*TADKA*)

2 tbsp oil

1 tsp black mustard seeds (*sarson seeds*), 8-10 curry leaves (*curry patta*)

3 whole dry red chillies

1. Make a paste of the onion, ginger and garlic in a blender.

2. Heat the oil in a *kadhai*, add onion paste from blender and green chillies. Cook until onion turns brown.

3. Add red chilli powder, coriander powder, garam masala and salt. Mix. Cook on medium heat until oil separates. Sprinkle a little water if the masala sticks to the pan.

4. Add tamarind pulp, coconut milk and 1 cup of water. Let it come to a boil. Add fish and cook on low heat for 10-12 minutes or until the fish is cooked. Remove from fire.

5. For the tempering, heat the oil in a frying pan add all the ingredients. When the seeds start spluttering pour over the hot fish. Serve hot.

Prawn Curry

A delicious, spicy prawn curry with coconut milk.

Serves 4-6

250 gm prawns - shelled, with tails intact

2 tbsp oil

¼ tsp red chilli paste, ½ tsp ground turmeric, 2 cups coconut milk

½ tsp salt, or to taste, ½ tsp sugar

4-5 cherry tomatoes or 125 gm regular tomatoes - cut into 1"/2.5 cm pieces

juice of 1 lemon (2 tbsp)

GARNISH

1-2 green/red chillies - chopped, some green coriander leaves

1. Heat oil. Add chilli paste and turmeric. Fry for 2 minutes till oil separates.

2. Add three fourth cup coconut milk. Boil, stirring constantly. Simmer for 5-7 minutes. Add salt and sugar. Add the rest of the coconut milk. Boil for 3-4 minutes.

3. Add prawns and tomatoes. Cook for 4-5 minutes till prawns are cooked and the gravy becomes thick. Add lemon juice. Mix.

4. Garnish with chopped chillies and coriander leaves. Serve hot with rice.

Vegetarian Main Course

Methi Malai Matar

Serves 3-4

100 gm cottage cheese (*paneer*) - cut into small ½" cubes, 1 cup peas

½ stick cinnamon (*dalchini*), 2 big cardamoms, 3-4 cloves (*laung*)

½ cup yogurt mixed with ¼ tsp white pepper powder, 1 tsp dhania powder

½ tsp red chilli powder, salt to taste, a pinch of sugar

2 tbsp cashewnuts (*kaju*) - powdered

4 tbsp oil, 3 onions - ground to a paste, 1 tbsp ginger-garlic paste

4 tbsp dry fenugreek leaves (*kasoori methi*)

4-5 tbsp cream

1. Crush together dalchini, laung and seeds of moti elaichi. Add the above spices and cashew nut powder to the yogurt. Add pepper, salt, sugar, dhania powder and red chilli powder. Whisk yogurt well till smooth.

2. Heat oil. Add ground onion and cook on low heat till very light golden and oil separates. Add the ginger garlic and stir till golden brown.

3. Add yogurt and stir on low heat for 3-4 minutes till oil separates. Add kasoori methi and stir for 2 minutes. Add 1 cup hot water and simmer for 2-3 minutes. Add boiled peas and paneer. Add enough cream to get a thick gravy. Serve.

Paneer Makhani

Paneer is added to a fragrant tomato curry cooked in butter. You may substitute paneer with potatoes and peas if you like and turn it into makhani aloo matar.

Serves 6

250 gm *paneer* - cut into 1"/2.5 cm pieces

GRAVY

3 tbsp butter or oil

2 onions - chopped (1 cup), 1 tsp chopped ginger

½ tsp red chilli powder, 6-7 tomatoes (500 gm) - chopped

¼ cup yogurt - whisked till smooth

3 tbsp cashews (*kaju*) - soaked in a little water for 15 minutes & ground to a paste

¼ tsp ground nutmeg, optional, 1½ tsp salt, or to taste, ¾ tsp garam masala

½-1 tsp sugar, or to taste, ½ cup thin fresh cream or milk

1 tbsp tomato ketchup

1. Heat 2 tbsp butter or oil in a pan. Add onions and ginger. Cook on low heat until onions turn transparent. Add red chilli powder. Stir. Add chopped tomatoes. Cover and cook for 7-8 minutes till the tomatoes turn pulpy.

2. Add yogurt. Cook till the mixture turns dry and reddish again.

3. Remove from heat. Cool. Grind to a very smooth puree with ½ cup water. Heat 1 tbsp of butter or oil in a wok or a deep pan. Add the prepared tomato-yogurt puree. Stir fry for 3-4 minutes on low heat.

4. Add salt, garam masala, sugar and tomato ketchup. Mix. Add cashew paste. Cook on low heat for 1-2 minutes.

5. Add enough milk or very thin fresh cream, to get a thick pouring consistency of the gravy. Add *paneer* pieces. Give one boil on low heat. Remove from heat. Transfer to a serving dish.

6. Garnish with a swirl of cream, a few coriander leaves and ginger match-sticks. Serve with *nans, paranthas* or any other bread.

Paalak Paneer

Serves 4

½ kg paalak (spinach), choose a bundle with smaller leaves

3 tbsp oil, 1 moti illaichi (brown cardamom)

2-3 laung (cloves), 3-4 saboot kali mirch (peppercorns), 3 onions - chopped

1" piece ginger - chopped, 4-6 flakes garlic - chopped, 1 green chilli - chopped

1 tbsp kasoori methi (dried fenugreek leaves), ¾ tsp garam masala

½ tsp red chilli powder, ¼ tsp amchoor, 1¼ tsp salt, or to taste

2 tomatoes - chopped, 100 gms paneer (cottage cheese) - cut into 1" cubes

BAGHAR (TEMPERING)

1 tbsp desi ghee or butter, 1" piece ginger - cut into thin long pieces

1 green chilli - slit into long pieces, ½ tsp red chilli powder

1. Break paalak leaves into small pieces. Discard stalks. Wash in plenty of water. Keep aside to drain.

2. Heat oil in a kadhai. Add moti illaichi, laung and saboot kali mirch.

3. Add chopped onions and cook till light brown.

4. Add ginger, garlic & green chillies. Stir on low flame for 1 minute. Add kasoori methi.

5. Add garam masala, red chilli powder, amchoor and salt. Stir on low flame for 1 minute.

6. Add chopped tomatoes. Cook for 3-4 minutes, till well blended.

7. Add spinach and cook uncovered for 10-12 minutes on low flame. Remove from fire. Cool.

8. Blend the cooled mixture along with ½ cup water, just for a few seconds, to a coarse paste. Do not grind it too finely.

9. Boil 1 cup water & add the spinach paste to it. Simmer, covered for 4-5 minutes.

10. Cut paneer into 1" cubes, leaving aside some for garnishing. Deep fry to a golden colour.

11. Mix paneer pieces in the cooked spinach. Give it one boil. Simmer for 2-3 minutes till paneer turns soft. Transfer to a serving dish.

12. Heat 1 tbsp desi ghee or butter. Add ginger and green chilli. Remove from fire. Add red chilli powder and pour oil on the hot paalak. Mix lightly. Serve.

Note: You can forget frying the paneer if you wish!

Dal Makhani

Serves 4-5

1 cup whole black beans (*urad sabut*)

2 tbsp red kidney beans (*rajma*)

1 tbsp *channe ki dal,* 2 tbsp desi ghee

1½ tsp salt, 5 cups of water, 1 cup ready-made tomato puree

¼ tsp jaiphal powder, ½ tsp garam masala

1½ tbsp dry fenugreek leaves (*kasoori methi*)

2-3 tbsp butter, preferably white

GRIND TO A PASTE

2 dry, whole red chillies, preferably Kashmiri red chillies - deseeded & soaked for
10 minutes and then drained, 1" piece ginger, 6-8 flakes garlic

ADD LATER

½ cup milk mixed with ½ cup cream or well beaten malai

1. Wash the dals and red kidney beans, and soak in water overnight.

2. Drain water. Wash several times in fresh water, rubbing well, till the water get clear.

3. Pressure cook dal with 5 cups water, 2 tbsp ghee, salt and ginger-garlic-chilli paste. After the first whistle, keep on low flame for 30 minutes. Remove from fire. After the pressure drops, mash the hot dal a little. Keep aside.

4. To the dal in the cooker, add tomato puree, dry fenugreek leaves, garam masala and jaiphal powder.

5. Add butter. Simmer on medium flame for 20 minutes, stirring dal occasionally. Remove from fire. Keep aside to cool till the time of serving.

6. At the time of serving, add milk mixed with cream to the dal. Keep dal on fire and bring to a boil on low heat, stirring constantly. Mix very well with a *karchi*. Simmer for 2 minutes more, to get the right colour and smoothness. Remove from fire. Serve.

Note: Originally the dal was cooked by leaving it overnight on the burning coal angeethis. The longer the dal simmered, the better it tasted.

Kofta Rangeen

Potato dumplings (koftas) with colourful vegetable filling. The colours are exposed by dividing each kofta into two. Served on a bed of red, cardamom flavoured curry.

Serves 4

KOFTA COVERING

4 slices bread - dipped in water & squeezed, 4 potatoes - boiled & grated (2 cups)

¾ tsp salt, or to taste, ½ tsp black pepper, pinch of baking powder, 2 tsp tomato ketchup

KOFTA FILLING

1 carrot - grated thickly (½ cup), 1 capsicum - shredded (½ cup)

3-4 tbsp shredded green cabbage, ¼ cup grated cheddar cheese, salt, pepper to taste

GRAVY

4 tbsp oil, 2 black cardamoms (*moti illaichi*), 2 onions - chopped (1 cup)

3 tomatoes - chopped (1½ cups), 2 tsp finely grated ginger

1½ tsp ground coriander (*dhania powder*), ½ tsp each red chilli powder & garam masala

¾ cup milk, 1 tbsp tomato ketchup, salt to taste

1. To prepare the kofta covering, in a bowl mix all the ingredients given under kofta covering till well blended. Divide into 4 big balls. Keep aside. For the filling, mix all the vegetables with cheese together. Sprinkle some salt and pepper to taste. Flatten each potato ball to a size of about 3"/8 cm diameter. Place 1 tbsp of filling in the centre. Lift the sides to cover the filling.

2. Give the kofta an oval shape like an egg. Deep fry koftas, one at a time, carefully to a golden brown colour.

3. To prepare the gravy, grind onions, tomatoes and ginger together. Heat oil. Add cardamoms and wait for 30-40 seconds. Add onion-tomato paste and cook on medium heat till well dried. Add ground coriander and red chilli powder. Stir fry till oil comes to the surface.

4. Reduce heat. Add milk gradually, 2-3 tbsp at a time, stirring continuously. Cook on low heat till the mixture turns red again and the oil separates. Add enough water to get a thin curry. Boil. Add salt, garam masala, tomato ketchup and cook on low heat for 8-10 minutes till it thickens slightly. Keep aside.

5. To serve, cut koftas into two. Boil the gravy separately, and pour in a serving dish. Arrange the koftas on the gravy and microwave for a couple of minutes to heat the koftas. Serve immediately with rice or bread.

Mushroom and Pea Curry

Mushrooms and peas are simmered in a delicious thick curry, flavoured with whole spices.

Serves 4

200 gm button mushrooms - trimmed and cut into quarters (2 cups) or

1 cup tinned mushrooms

½ cup boiled or frozen peas

3 tbsp oil, 1 tbsp butter

½ tsp cumin seeds (*jeera*), 1 bay leaf (*tej patta*)

2 black cardamoms (*moti illaichi*), 2 cloves (*laung*)

2 onions - chopped finely (1 cup), 1½ tsp ground coriander (*dhania powder*)

½ tsp red chilli powder, ½ tsp garam masala

¼ tsp ground turmeric (*haldi*), ¼ tsp dry mango powder (*amchoor*)

1¼ tsp salt, or to taste

2 pinches each of pepper and sugar

¼ cup tomato puree

2 tbsp cashews (*kaju*) ground to a paste with 3 tbsp water

1½ cups milk

1. Boil 2-3 cups water with 1 tsp salt. Add chopped mushrooms. After the boil comes again, keep on heat for a minute. Remove from heat and drain the water. Add fresh water and strain again. Keep aside.

2. Heat butter. Add the mushrooms and saute for 2-3 minutes on medium heat till water evaporates. Add the peas. Add 2 pinches each of salt, pepper and sugar. Stir for 2 minutes and keep aside.

3. Heat oil in a heavy bottomed pan. Add cumin, bay leaf, cardamoms and cloves. When cumin turns golden, add onions and stir fry till light golden.

4. Reduce heat. Add ground coriander, red chilli powder, garam masala, turmeric, mango powder and salt. Stir fry till onions turn golden brown.

5. Add tomato puree. Cook on low heat for about 5 minutes till oil surfaces. Add cashew paste and stir to mix well. Add milk, stirring continuously. Stir till it boils.

6. Add mushrooms and peas. Boil. Cover and simmer on low heat for 8-10 minutes, till oil surfaces and the gravy turns thick. Serve hot with breads like *chappatis* or *nans*.

Chutneys & Pickles

Garlic Pickle

A very easy pickle to prepare. It helps in also digesting the food besides adding zest to the food.

Makes 500 gm

½ kg garlic - peeled

½ cup mustard oil

½ cup vinegar

25 gm (5 tsp) salt

2 tsp ground turmeric (*haldi*)

4 tsp red chilli powder

4 tsp ground mustard (*rai*)

1. Peel the garlic. Heat mustard oil to smoking point. Reduce heat. Add all the garlic together. Cook for 2 minutes on low heat. Let it cool.

2. Heat vinegar in a separate pan. Remove from heat. Add salt, turmeric, red chilli powder and ground mustard.

3. Mix the garlic in oil to the *masalas* in vinegar. Fill it in dry bottles. This pickle can be eaten immediately also.

Hari Chutney

*A green (hari) chutney prepared front fresh coriander and mint leaves.
As long as this chutney is there with my meals, I can enjoy anything
without creating a fuss. My favourite!*

Serves 4

½ cup mint leaves *(pudina leaves)*

1 cup fresh coriander *(hara dhania)* - chopped along with stems

2 green chillies, 1 onion - chopped (½ cup)

1½ tsp dried mango powder *(amchoor)*

1½ tsp sugar

½ tsp salt, or to taste

1. Wash coriander and mint leaves. Grind all the ingredients together to a smooth paste. Serve with snacks or with meals.

Coconut & Peanut Chutney

*This authentic chutney, originating from Southern India, is superb with all types of bean
and lentil appetizers. Fresh coconut is traditional, but to make the procedure
simpler, you may opt for the desiccated coconut instead.*

Serves 6

½ cup freshly grated or desiccated coconut

½ cup roasted peanuts (without the red skin)

1 green chilli - chopped, 1 onion - chopped (½ cup)

½ tsp salt, or to taste, ½"/1 cm piece ginger, 1 cup yogurt - approx.

TEMPERING

1 tbsp oil, 1 tsp mustard seeds *(sarson)*

1-2 dry, red chillies - broken into bits, a few curry leaves

1. Grind all ingredients of the chutney adding enough curd to get a thick paste of soft dropping consistency. Keep aside in a bowl.

2. To temper the chutney, heat 1 tbsp oil. Add mustard seeds. When they splutter, add broken red chillies and curry leaves. Remove from heat and pour the tempered oil on the chutney. Mix lightly.

Gobhi Shalgam ka Achaar

Make up your mind to pickle seasonal vegetables and enjoy them throughout the year.

Makes 2 kg

2½ kg - cauliflower (*gobi*), carrots and shalgam (all 3 vegetables mixed together)

100 gm garlic - ground to a paste, 100 gm ginger - ground to paste

100 gm ground mustard (*rai powder*), 3-4 tsp turmeric (*haldi*)

100 gm red chillies (for a hot pickle, add more chillies)

500 gm jaggery (*gur*), 2 cups (500 ml) white vinegar

500 gm mustard oil, 25 gm dried fenugreek leaves (*kasoori methi*), 100 gm salt

1. Peel carrots and shalgam (turnips). Cut carrots into fingers, shalgam into round slices and gobi (cauliflower) into medium sized florets. Boil water in a big pan. Add vegetables. Remove from fire immediately. Let the vegetables be in the hot water for about 5 minutes. Keep aside.

2. Remove the vegetables from the water with a slotted spoon and dry them on a clean cloth in the shade.

3. Next day, heat oil to smoking point, reduce flame. Add garlic paste and fry till light golden. Add ginger paste and fry till light brown. Remove from fire.

4. Add salt, mustard powder, dried fenugreek leaves, red chilli powder and turmeric to the ginger-garlic mixture. Smear the dried vegetables kept in a large pan, with this masala and transfer them in a jar.

5. In a clean dry pan heat vinegar, add gur to it and cook till gur dissolves. Strain it, cool and add it to the pickle in the jar. Shake well so that it mixes evenly with the vegetables. Keep the pickle in the sun for 4-5 days.

Note:

1. If you want the pickle to be sweet, reduce the chillies and increase the gur according to taste.

2. If you like the pickle to be soft, boil the vegetables for 2-3 minutes and then remove from fire.

Rice & Breads

Minty Chicken Biryani

Rice cooked with chicken and flavoured with fresh mint.

Serves 8

2 cups basmati rice - cleaned & soaked in water for 30 minutes

8 pieces chicken of 2"/5 cm size, ½ cup mint (*pudina*) leaves - finely chopped

4 tbsp oil or ghee, ½ tsp black cumin seeds (*shah jeera*), 1 bay leaf (*tej patta*)

2 onions - finely sliced (1 cup), 2 tomatoes - finely chopped (1 cup)

½ tsp chilli powder, 1 tsp garam masala, salt to taste

BOIL TOGETHER

5 cups water, 1 cinnamon (*dalchini*) stick, 4 cloves (*laung*)

4 black cardamoms (*moti illaichi*), 1"/2.5 cm piece ginger - chopped

1. Boil 5 cups of water with whole spices and ginger. Add chicken and cook until chicken turns just tender. Remove from heat, strain and keep aside the chicken pieces and the stock separately. Discard the whole spices and ginger.

2. Heat oil or ghee in a large, heavy bottomed pan. Add black cumin seeds and a bay leaf. After 30 seconds, add sliced onions and fry until golden brown.

3. Add chicken pieces, chopped tomato and mint leaves. Saute until chicken turns light brown. Add the red chilli powder, garam masala and salt.

4. Add 4 cups of chicken stock. Add the drained rice. Bring to a boil, cover and cook on low heat for about 14-15 minutes or until all the water is absorbed and the rice is done. Serve hot with a refreshing raita.

South Indian Lemon Rice

Yellow rice flavoured with mustard seeds and lemon juice. Ground turmeric is used to give colour to it. Yellow split peas add crunch to the rice.

Serves 4

1 cup basmati rice

juice of 2 lemons (3 tbsp), ¼ tsp ground turmeric (*haldi*)

½ tsp sugar, 1½ tsp salt, or to taste

TEMPERING

3 tbsp oil

1 tsp mustard seeds (*sarson*), 1 tbsp yellow split peas (*channe ki dal*)

3 dry, red chillies - broken into pieces, few curry leaves

1. Clean and wash rice. Boil 5-6 cups water in a large pan. Add rice. Boil for 7-8 minutes till just done. Strain the rice. Cool for ½ hour by spreading rice on a tray. Separate the rice grains with a fork.

2. Mix lemon juice, turmeric, salt and sugar together. Keep aside.

3. Heat oil in a large wok. Reduce heat. Add mustard seeds, yellow split peas and red chillies. Cook on very low heat till split peas turn brown. Add curry leaves.

4. Add the lemon juice mixture. Add ¼ cup water. Cover and simmer on low heat till split peas turn soft and the water dries. Run a fork through the boiled rice to separate the rice grains and add the rice to the lemon juice mixture in the wok. Stir gently to mix well. Serve hot with yogurt.

Spinach Parantha

Chopped spinach and flour, flavoured with some carom seeds are kneaded together to a dough. A pinch of turmeric added to the dough makes the parantha more pleasing to the eyes.

Serves 4

2½ cups whole wheat flour (*atta*)

1½ cups finely chopped spinach

1 tsp salt

½ tsp turmeric (*haldi*), ½ tsp red chilli powder

½ tsp garam masala, ¾ tsp carom seeds (*ajwain*)

ghee or oil for frying

1. Wash spinach leaves and place them in a shallow pan or a food processor. Add all other ingredients except the flour and ghee for frying.

2. Add the flour on top. Mix well. Add just enough water to make a firm dough of rolling consistency. Knead well till smooth and elastic. Cover and keep aside for at least 30 minutes for the dough to become soft and elastic.

3. Take small portions of the dough, roll them out into round chapatis and smear with ghee. Fold into half. Again fold into half to form a triangle. Roll out once more to a big triangular *parantha*.

4. Put one *parantha* at a time on a heated *tawa* (griddle), cook one side and turn over. Add a little ghee from the sides and some on the top surface. Turn and cook till it gets a nice brown colour. Cook on medium heat. When ready it should be crisp. Similarly, make more *paranthas*.

Keema Parantha

Serves 8

250 gm minced meat (*keema*)

1 onion - chopped finely

2 tsp finely chopped ginger

1 tsp salt, 1 tsp coriander powder (*dhania*), ½ tsp red chilli powder, ½ tsp garam masala

2 green chillies - chopped, 1 tbsp finely chopped fresh coriander

1 tbsp dry fenugreek leaves (*kasoori methi*)

DOUGH

2 cups wheat flour (*atta*), ½ tsp salt, 1 tbsp ghee

1. To prepare the dough, sift flour and salt. Rub 1 tbsp ghee. Add enough water to make a dough. Keep aside for 30 minutes.

2. To prepare the filling, heat 2 tbsp of oil and fry the chopped onions until rich brown.

3. Add mince and ginger and mix well. Reduce heat. Add salt, coriander powder, red chilli powder and garam masala. Fry for 1-2 minutes. Cook covered on low heat for about 5-7 minutes, till the mince is cooked.

4. Add green chillies and 1 tbsp finely chopped coriander. If there is any water, uncover and dry the mince on fire. Keep the stuffing aside.

5. Divide the dough into 6 equal parts. Shape into round balls.

6. Flatten each ball, roll out each into a round of 5" diameter.

7. Spread 1 tsp full of ghee. Then spread 2 tbsp of filling all over.

8. Make a slit, starting from the centre till any one end.

9. Start rolling from the slit, to form an even cone.

10. Keeping the cone upright, press slightly.

11. Roll out, applying pressure only at the centre. Do not roll or press too much on the sides, otherwise the layers of parantha do not separate after cooking.

12. Sprinkle some kasoori methi and press with a rolling pin (*belan*).

13. Apply water on the back side of the parantha and stick carefully in a heated tandoor or place in a preheated oven in a greased tray. Remove after a few minutes. Spread some ghee, serve hot.

Murg Pullao

Serves 4

1 cup basmati rice - washed & soaked in 2 cups water for 30 minutes

250 gm chicken - cut into pieces

¾ tsp salt, ½ tsp turmeric powder (*haldi*)

PASTE

3 dried, red chillies - deseeded

2 onions - chopped

3 tbsp oil

12-14 flakes garlic, 2 tsp chopped ginger

1 tbsp cumin seeds (*jeera*), 2 tsp fennel (*saunf*)

1 tsp salt

1" stick cinnamon (*dalchini*)

seeds of 2 black cardamoms (*moti illaichi*)

3 cloves (*laung*)

8 peppercorns (*saboot kali mirch*)

1. Soak rice in 2 cups water for 30 minutes. For the paste grind all ingredients together, using some water.

2. Heat oil in a *kadhai*. Add paste cook for 1 minute.

3. Add chicken cook for 3-4 minutes.

4. Add rice along with the water. Add salt and turmeric. Mix gently. Bring to a boil, cover and cook on low heat until all the water is absorbed and the rice is done for about 10-12 minutes. Serve hot with a refreshing raita.

Subz Biryani

The term biryani is used to define a fragrant rice preparation which was very popular in the Moghul era. This vegetable rice is cooked with a fragrant biryani paste made from many flavourful seeds. Remember to cook biryani in a large, heavy bottomed pan.

Serves 6-8

2 cups basmati rice - soaked in water for 1 hour

100 gm carrots - cut into small cubes, 300 gm cauliflower - cut into small florets

10 french beans - cut into small pieces, 2 onions - sliced finely (1 cup)

1/3 cup oil, 3 tsp salt, or to taste, 1 tsp lemon juice, 1 bay leaf (*tej patta*)

BIRYANI PASTE

6-7 flakes garlic, 1"/2.5 cm piece ginger

1 tsp fennel seeds (*saunf*), 1 tsp cumin seeds (*jeera*), 1 tsp ground coriander (*dhania*)

1 stick of cinnamon (*dalchini*), 3 cloves (*laung*)

seeds of 2 green cardamoms (*chhoti illaichi*)

1. Grind all the ingredients of the biryani paste together with a little water. Keep paste aside. Heat oil in a large, heavy bottomed pan. Add onions, cook till golden brown.

2. Add the ground biryani paste. Stir fry on low heat for 1-2 minutes. Add the vegetables and stir fry for 2-3 minutes.

3. Measure 4 cups of water (double the volume of rice) and add to the vegetables. Add salt and lemon juice. When water boils, drain the rice and add to the boiling water. Give it a boil. Reduce heat.

4. Cover the pan of rice with a small towel napkin and then with a well fitting lid. Keep some heavy weight on the lid. To reduce heat further, you may put a heavy griddle under the pan of rice. Cook for about 12-15 minutes, or until the rice is done. Fluff the rice with a fork, so that the grains separate. Serve after 10 minutes with plain yogurt.

Afghani Nan

Nans are oblong oven baked flat breads. Traditionally they are baked in a clay oven called 'tandoor' but I have prepared them in an electric boiler with equal success.

Serves 4

2 cups (250 gm) plain flour (*maida*)

½ cup hot milk

½ tsp baking powder

½ cup warm water (approx.)

½ tsp salt

1 tsp nigella seeds (*kalaunji*) or 1 tsp black or white sesame seeds (*til*)

1. Heat milk and put it in a large, shallow pan or a mixing bowl. Add baking powder to the hot milk. Mix well and keep it undisturbed for 1 minute. Bubbles will start appearing on the surface.

2. Sift plain flour and salt together. Add flour to the hot milk in the pan or bowl. Mix well. Knead to a soft dough with enough warm water. Keep in a warm place for 3-4 hours to swell.

3. At serving time, make 6-8 balls of the dough. Roll out each ball to an oblong shape. Sprinkle some onion seeds or sesame seeds. Press the seeds with a rolling pin. Pull one side of the nan to give it a pointed end like the shape of the nan.

4. Apply some water on the back side of the nan. Press on the walls of a hot tandoor. Alternatively, cover the rack of the oven with an aluminium foil. Bake the nans in a very hot oven or broiler by keeping them on the foil. When light brown specs appear on the surface, turn the side of all the nans. Cook till done. Smear some butter on the hot nan and serve hot with *dals* or curries.

Desserts & Puddings

Malpua

These pancakes are soaked in syrup, making them one of the best desserts for people with a sweet tooth. Prepare the batter at least one hour before frying the malpuas.

Makes 20-24 small malpuas

BATTER

1 cup flour (*maida*), 2 tbsp whole wheat flour (*atta*)

1 tsp fennel (*saunf*) - crushed, seeds of 2 green cardamoms (*chhoti illaichi*) - crushed

1 cup *malai* - keep in the strainer for 1 hour

¼ cup milk, optional, ghee for frying

SUGAR SYRUP

1 cup sugar, ½ cup water, a few strands saffron or 1-2 drops yellow food colour

2 green cardamoms (*chhoti illaichi*)

1. Mix both flours with malai so that no lumps remain. The batter should be of a thick, soft consistency, like a cake batter. Add a little milk if needed. A thin batter will spread. Add fennel and cardamoms. Leave aside for 1-2 hours (important).

2. Heat ghee for deep frying in a nonstick frying pan. With the help of a spoon drop a spoonful of batter in moderately hot ghee. Spread with a spoon to get a small round malpua. Put as many (about 2-3) malpuas as the pan can hold.

3. Reduce heat. Fry malpuas in oil for about 4-5 minutes on low heat till golden brown on both sides. Drain and keep aside.

4. Mix sugar, water and all other ingredients for sugar syrup in a pan. Boil for 5-6 minutes to get one thread consistency syrup (*ek taar ki chaashni*). Remove from fire. Drop malpuas in hot sugar syrup, 2-3 at a time. Give 1-2 boils. Remove with a slotted spoon so that excess syrup is drained. Place on a serving dish and garnish with chopped almonds and pistas. Serve plain or with rabri or kheer.

Note: Malpuas can be fried in advance and kept without sugar syrup in an airtight box in the fridge for 1-2 days. At the time of serving drop into hot sugar syrup, give 1-2 boils and serve hot.

Besan ki Burfi

Makes 24 pieces

250 gm (2¾ cups) gramflour (*besan*), 150 gm (1 cup) powdered sugar

150 gm (¾ cup) pure ghee, 3-4 green cardamoms (*chhoti illaichi*) - powder

1. In a heavy bottomed pan, put gramflour. Dry roast gramflour for about 10 minutes on low heat, stirring continuously till it becomes fragrant and gives out a roasted smell.

2. Add ghee. Cook on very low heat for about 15 minutes till the gramflour turns golden. Do not make it brown. Make it just golden with a hint of brown.

3. Remove from fire. Add sugar and mix well.

4. Transfer to a greased *thali*. Press well to make the top smooth.

5. Sprinkle green cardamom powder. Leave to set for 5-6 hours at room temperature in a cool place but not in the refrigerator. You can leave it over night to set well.

6. Cut into 1" squares and store in an air tight box after it turns absolutely cold.

Note: To make besan laddoo, increase the besan to 3 cups.

Kesari Phirni

A milk pudding cooked with ground rice paste and flavoured with saffron and green cardamoms.

Serves 6

3½ cups (700 gm) milk, 1/3 cup basmati rice

1/3 cup sugar (slightly less than ½ cup) or to taste

25 almonds - blanched and ground to a paste with some water

4 almonds (*badam*) - shredded

5-6 green pistachios (*pista*) - soaked, peeled and sliced

2 small silver leaves - optional

seeds of 2-3 green cardamoms (*chhoti illaichi*) - powder

1 drop kewra essence or 1 tsp ruh kewra

a pinch of yellow colour

DECORATION

a few rose petals - dipped in cold water, a few strands kesar - soaked in warm water

a few fresh anaar ke daane

1. Soak rice of good quality for about 2-3 hours and then grind very fine with 4 to 5 tablespoonfuls of cold water to a paste. (You may soak rice overnight and keep in the fridge.)

2. Dissolve the rice paste in ½ cup milk and make it thin.

3. Mix the rice paste with the remaining 3 cups milk in a heavy bottomed pan. Keep on fire and cook on medium heat, stirring continuously, till the mixture is of creamy consistency, about 5 minutes.

4. Add the kesar water or a drop of colour, sugar and cardamom powder and stir. Simmer till sugar is fully dissolved and then boil for 5-6 minutes on medium heat.

5. Remove from fire. Add almond paste. Mix well.

6. Add ruh kewra or the essence and half of the shredded almonds and pistachios.

7. Pour the mixture into 6 small earthern containers. Chill. Decorate each dish with a silver leaf, rose petals, kesar and the remaining shredded nuts. Top with some fresh anaar ke daane.

Saffron Kulfi Falooda

The delicious Indian Ice cream topped with sweetened thin vermicelli.
Saffron lends it's flavour and colour to this most popular Indian dessert.
Pistachios and almonds add to the richness.

Serves 6-8

1 kg (5 cups) full fat milk

5 tbsp skimmed milk powder, 3 tbsp cornflour

¼ cup sugar, 6-7 strands saffron (*kesar*)

3-4 green cardamoms (*chhoti illaichi*) - crushed, 1 tbsp shredded pistachios (*pista*)

1 tbsp shredded almonds (*badam*)

FALOODA

1 cup thin rice vermicelli, 3-4 strands saffron (*kesar*)

3 tbsp sugar, 2 green cardamoms (*chhoti illaichi*)

1. Dissolve cornflour and milk powder in ½ cup milk to a paste. Heat the rest of the milk with sugar and saffron. Add the paste gradually, stirring continuously. Mix well. Add crushed seeds of green cardamoms. Boil. Simmer on low heat, for about 15 minutes till slightly thick.

2. Cool. Add pistachios and almonds. Fill in clean kulfi moulds and leave to set in the freezer for 6-8 hours or overnight.

3. To prepare the falooda boil 4 cups water. Add the rice vermicelli. Boil. Simmer on low heat for 2-3 minutes till the vermicelli turns soft and no crunch remains. Strain. Add cold water to refresh. Strain again.

4. Make a sugar syrup by boiling ¾ cup water, 3 tbsp sugar, saffron and green cardamoms together. Simmer for a couple of minutes. Remove from heat and put in the boiled vermicelli. Keep soaked in sugar syrup, in the refrigerator, till serving time.

5. To serve, remove the kulfi from the mould, cut into two halves lengthways and top with some falooda (without the syrup). Serve.

Gajar ka Halwa

Almost every home in India has a box stocked with this carrot pudding in winters. It is served hot during the cold winter months, when fresh, red carrots are in plenty.

Serves 4

500 gm carrots - grated into long shreds

1 cup milk

¼ cup sugar

2-3 tbsp ghee or unsalted butter

5-6 almonds (*badam*) - shredded

10-12 raisins (*kishmish*)

seeds of 3 green cardamoms (*illaichi*) - crushed

100 gm khoya - grated

1. Boil milk with crushed cardamom seeds in a clean wok or a deep pan. Add grated carrots and cook uncovered, stirring occasionally, till milk dries.

2. Add almonds and raisins. Stir for 1 minute. Add sugar. Cook till the mixture turns dry again.

3. Add ghee and stir fry for 10 minutes on low heat till ghee separates.

4. Add khoya and mix well for 2-3 minutes. Serve hot garnished with some nuts.

INTERNATIONAL CONVERSION GUIDE

These are not exact equivalents; they've been rounded-off to make measuring easier.

WEIGHTS & MEASURES

Metric	Imperial
15 g	½ oz
30 g	1 oz
60 g	2 oz
90 g	3 oz
125 g	4 oz (¼ lb)
155 g	5 oz
185 g	6 oz
220 g	7 oz
250 g	8 oz (½ lb)
280 g	9 oz
315 g	10 oz
345 g	11 oz
375 g	12 oz (¾ lb)
410 g	13 oz
440 g	14 oz
470 g	15 oz
500 g	16 oz (1 lb)
750 g	24 oz (1½ lb)
1 kg	30 oz (2 lb)

LIQUID MEASURES

Metric	Imperial
30 ml	1 fluid oz
60 ml	2 fluid oz
100 ml	3 fluid oz
125 ml	4 fluid oz
150 ml	5 fluid oz (¼ pint/1 gill)
190 ml	6 fluid oz
250 ml	8 fluid oz
300 ml	10 fluid oz (½ pint)
500 ml	16 fluid oz
600 ml	20 fluid oz (1 pint)
1000 ml	1¾ pints

CUPS & SPOON MEASURES

Metric	Imperial
1 ml	¼ tsp
2 ml	½ tsp
5 ml	1 tsp
15 ml	1 tbsp
60 ml	¼ cup
125 ml	½ cup
250 ml	1 cup

HELPFUL MEASURES

Metric	Imperial
3 mm	1/8 in
6 mm	¼ in
1 cm	½ in
2 cm	¾ in
2.5 cm	1 in
5 cm	2 in
6 cm	2½ in
8 cm	3 in
10 cm	4 in
13 cm	5 in
15 cm	6 in
18 cm	7 in
20 cm	8 in
23 cm	9 in
25 cm	10 in
28 cm	11 in
30 cm	12 in (1 ft)

HOW TO MEASURE

When using the graduated metric measuring cups, it is important to shake the dry ingredients loosely into the required cup. Do not tap the cup on the table, or pack the ingredients into the cup unless otherwise directed. Level top of cup with a knife. When using graduated metric measuring spoons, level top of spoon with a knife. When measuring liquids in the jug, place jug on a flat surface, check for accuracy at eye level.

OVEN TEMPERATURE

These oven temperatures are only a guide. Always check the manufacturer's manual.

	°C (Celsius)	°F (Fahrenheit)	Gas Mark
Very low	120	250	1
Low	150	300	2
Moderately low	160	325	3
Moderate	180	350	4
Moderately high	190	375	5
High	200	400	6
Very high	230	450	7